IN A NUTSHELL

More can be said
in fewer words
in verse
But more important
More can be heard.

PRESTWICK PUBLISHING CO.
P.O. Box 90277
1277 Garnet Avenue
San Diego, California 92109-0780

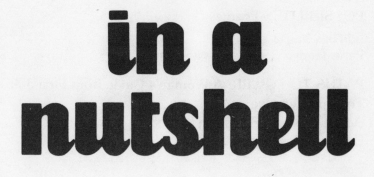

in a nutshell

Feminine Verse

ist

by

Natasha Josefowitz

PRESTWICK PUBLISHING CO.

Also by Natasha Josefowitz:

POSSIBILITÉS Poèmes
Editions Sagile
Paris, France, 1950

**PATHS TO POWER: A Woman's Guide from First Job
To Top Executive**
Addison-Wesley Publishing Company
Reading, Massachusetts 1980

Collaborator:
EFFECTIVE BEHAVIOR IN ORGANIZATIONS *Revised*
Richard D. Irwin
Homewood, Illinois 1980

Some of these poems have previously appeared in the following
publications:

**Paths to Power: A Woman's Guide from First Job to
Top Executive**
Natasha Josefowitz
Addison-Wesley Publishing Co.
Reading, Massachusetts 1980

The Androgenous Manager
Alice Sargent
American Management Association
New York, New York, 1981

The OD Practioner, *Vol. 13 #3, September 1981*

Glamour Magazine, *October 1980*

New Hampshire Magazine, *Vol. 6 #2, December 1977*

TABLE OF CONTENTS

WOMEN in the WORLD OF WORK

WOMEN and their IMPORTANT RELATIONSHIPS

IMPORTANT RELATIONSHIPS (continued)

WOMEN ALONE

To Herman

WOMEN
in the
WORLD
OF WORK

MY TYPIST

I talk into the tape machine
sometimes from an outline
other times from the heart.
From the outline
    it's better organized
from the heart
    is the passion.
She picks up the tape
    and in a few days
returns with the typewritten pages
    my manuscript!
I never quite recognize myself
    and seem to either
love it so much I can't change a line
or hate it so I want to throw it out.
But with it, comes each time
some special shiny fragment:
    my typist's comments
what she liked, what she didn't
    and why.
Her own life unfolds thru <u>her</u> pages
    and we touch each other
silently, secretly.

STEREOTYPES

She said to him
The academic life must be pleasant
you're a professor, how nice
He said to her
well, maybe some day
you'll marry one
She said to him
why should I marry one
when I can be one!

THE INTERVIEW

—Are you married?
—Well, yes.
—And do you have children?
—No —no we don't.
—Aren't you planning to?
  after all, you're a <u>young</u> woman!
—No, we're not planning children now.
—Well, even if you're not planning, they'll come
  and we would have trained you for nothing . . .
—No, we're not planning children and
  I'm very committed to a career.
—What methods of contraception do you use?

—What method does your company
  suggest to its employees?

SHE WHO GETS HIRED

She who gets hired
Is not necessarily the one
Who can do that job best
But the one who knows
The most about
How to get hired.

MY BOSS WINKED AT ME

My boss winked at me today
First I was pleased
it's a friendly thing to do
and then I wasn't
would he have winked at a man
NO
A wink is something men do
mostly to women
like little pats
wherever
Does it mean I'm cute
but not to be taken seriously
does it mean he likes me
but won't trust me
won't give me responsibility
won't promote me
won't give me raises
Hmmm
tomorrow
I'll wink at him

DID I SOUND OK?

Fifty people at the meeting —
I want to say something,
But is it relevant
And, is it pertinent
And, is this the time
Or should I wait?
Perhaps it is dumb.
Or has been said?
I wish it were not so important
for me to sound clever
and original
whenever I talk
wanting every time
to make an important contribution
to the goings on.
I hate wanting others
to respect me
I hate caring so much
that I should be liked
why should it matter
But it does,
Damn it, it <u>does!</u>
So with pounding heart
I say it — — —

Was it O.K.?
Tell me — how did I sound?

IMPRESSIONS FROM AN OFFICE

The family picture is on HIS desk.

Ah, a solid responsible family man.

HIS desk is cluttered.

He's obviously a hard worker and busy man.

HE is talking with his co-workers.

He must be discussing the latest deal.

HE'S not at his desk.

He must be at a meeting.

HE'S not in the office.

He's meeting customers.

HE'S having lunch with the boss.

He's on his way up.

The boss criticized HIM.

He'll improve his performance.

HE got an unfair deal.

Did he get angry?

HE'S getting married.

He'll get more settled.

HE'S having a baby.

He'll need a raise.

HE'S going on a business trip.

It's good for his career.

HE'S leaving for a better job.

He knows how to recognize a good opportunity.

The family picture is on HER desk.

Umm, her family will come before her career.

HER desk is cluttered.

She's obviously a disorganized scatterbrain.

SHE is talking with her co-workers.

She must be gossiping.

SHE'S not at her desk.

She must be in the ladies' room.

SHE'S not in the office.

She must be out shopping.

SHE'S having lunch with the boss.

They must be having an affair.

The boss criticized HER.

She'll be very upset.

SHE got an unfair deal.

Did she cry?

SHE'S getting married.

She'll get pregnant and leave.

SHE'S having a baby.

She'll cost the company money in maternity benefits.

SHE'S going on a business trip.

What does her husband say?

SHE'S leaving for a better job.

Women are undependable.

CONSULTING

The executive vice-president Robert Roth
took me to the board room
They sat at the long conference table
not wanting to listen to my proposal
I did not know how to start
how to make them hear
get them interested
and then the last man came in
and said, looking at me —
Hey, who's in charge here
and I said —
my name is Roberta Roth
I had a sex change operation
And I'm in charge here!
They listened.

THEORIES

The expert says this
The author writes that
The scholar knows this
The professor shows that
The leader promises this
The authority proclaims that
The researcher proves this
The statistician charts that

And I am confused
by <u>both</u> this and that

GOOD MANAGEMENT POTENTIAL

If I'm assertive
I'm seen as aggressive
If I'm aggressive
I'm a bitch
I won't be promoted

Let's try it again
If I'm non-assertive
I'm seen as a patsy
If I'm a patsy
I won't be promoted

Let's try it once more
If I'm very careful
I can go unnoticed
If I'm unnoticed
No one will know
I want to be promoted

Any suggestions?

BOYS WILL BE BOYS

A leer
A comment about her legs
A dirty joke
A brush against her
with an apology
A swear word
Oh, so sorry
A slur against women
that really wasn't meant that way
A conversation that stops
when she comes in
The whispering when she's there
The laughter when she passes by
The relief when she quits
Women just can't take it.
They have no sense of humour
and over react to a little "innocent fun"

SEXUAL HARASSMENT AT WORK

This is my assistant.
She's a great girl.

> I'm a woman, not a girl.

Look at her legs.
Hey, cutie!
What are you doing tonight?

> I'm busy.

How about a little hug
so I can feel those lovely breasts.
My wife is a cold fish
and a man needs some affection.

> Please stop.

If you come across, honey
I could do a lot for you.

> I don't have affairs
> with people I work with.

Oh, come on, don't be a prude.
I'll give you a real good time.

> Really, I'm not interested.

What's the matter, sweetheart.
You're playing hard to get.
I know you want it.

> You're wrong, leave me alone.

I know a horny little ass when I see one.

> Sigh

Let me feel it just a bit.

> Ouch!

Oh, that didn't hurt. You like it.

> Slap!

OK, if that's how you treat a man
who wants to help you in your career,
you're fired.

> But I do the job well and
> and I need the money.

Then if you know what's good for you
you'll take those panties off right now.

> Sob.

CHOICES

Up front
          or last row
Out there
          or hidden
Speaking up for
Speaking out against
          or shutting up
          into safety
Be heard
Visible
Criticized
Attacked
          Be quiet
          unnoticed
          left alone
          peaceful
To shout the anger
To cry the tears
To educate, correct, confront
          To mumble in corners
          grumble with friends
          protect myself from learning
          protect others from changing

THE BOSS'S SECRETARY

He pats her on the head
He sees it as fatherly
She sees it as demeaning

He tells her a dirty joke
He thinks it's funny
She thinks it's gross

He tells her she's cute
He thinks it's a compliment
She thinks "I'm not his daughter"

He asks her to sew on a button
He thinks she'll be glad to
She thinks "I'm not his mother"

He asks her to get him coffee
He thinks it's normal
She thinks "I'm not his servant"

He makes a pass at her
He thinks she'll enjoy it
She thinks "I'm not his sex object"

He asks her for a date
He thinks she will be flattered
She's afraid to refuse.

THE SUPERVISOR

I'm in charge of him
but she's in charge of me
She is in charge of him
but only through me.

I tell her his needs
I tell him her wants
He needs to work less
She wants him to work more.

And I'm in the middle.

HAND HOLDING

For many years I held
my teachers' hands
and I learned and learned.

Now my hand
is being held
and I teach and teach.

Isn't all this hand-holding wonderful?

TEACHING

Like an old amphora
I sit in the sands of time
Filled with the oil
of knowledge and experience

Like freshly baked claypots
they sit all around me
Filled with the pure waters
of youth and hope

If I pour my oil too gently
into the water-filled pots
It will stay on the surface
each untouched by the other

And so I vigorously shake
to make the two inseparable
For only when the water becomes heavier with knowledge
can the oil become lighter with joy

COMMUNICATIONS UPWARD

If I compliment my boss
He'll think I'm apple polishing
Trying to ingratiate myself.
The nasty word is: "A.K."

If I criticize my boss
He'll wonder: Who the hell does she think she is
Telling me what to do?
The words are: "the little bitch."

If I say nothing to my boss
He'll discount me as indifferent,
As a person without opinions.
The word is "invisible."

GONE ARE THE GOOD OLD DAYS!

When I patted her back
as I passed by her desk
she used to smile
now she says
"Don't touch me."

When I put my arm around her
and introduced her as "my girl"
she used to thank me
now she says
"I'm not your girl."

When I pinched her behind
as she leaned over to file
she used to giggle
now she says
"You are harassing me."

When I told her how I scored last night
she used to laugh
now she says
"I don't want to hear about it."

When I lied to my wife
about having to work late
she used to cover for me
now she refuses

When I asked her to do my shopping
she used to be delighted
now she says
"It's not in my job description."

LEADERSHIP

If the best of me can make more of you
then the best of you will reflect on me.

THE BOSS

I can only lead you well
    if you tell me how to best lead you.

I can make the best decisions
    only if you keep me informed.

I can prescribe best
    if you tell me the consequences.

I need to know
    my impact on you.

But I go beyond representing you
    beyond being your reflection.

I point out the way to new visions
    and to new paths for you to take.

THE NEW ETIQUETTE

He hires her
it is reverse discrimination
he doesn't
he's not complying with affirmative action.

He promotes her
he's playing favorites
he doesn't
he's sexist.

He opens the door for her
she doesn't need his help
he does not open the door
he's a boor.

He lights her cigarette
he's old fashioned
he doesn't
he's rude.

He picks up the dinner check
she's offended
he doesn't
he's stingy.

He greets her with a kiss
he's unprofessional
he doesn't
he's cold.

He gives her a raise
he has ulterior motives
he doesn't
he's a bastard.

EMPOWERMENT

First:
There must be power
which we feel

Next:
There must be power
which we wield

Then:
There can be power
which we share

TO BE POWERFUL ALWAYS

is
To FEEL powerful often
To ACT powerful sometimes
To OVERPOWER others seldom
To SHARE power whenever possible.

WHY NOT?

Sometimes confident
Sometimes scared
Sometimes in charge
Sometimes dependent
Sometimes tigress
Sometimes lamb
Sometimes Mother Goose
Sometimes Goldilocks
Wanting to be assertive
Afraid of the consequences
Wanting to be feminine
Afraid of the powerlessness
Wanting male prerogatives
Afraid to compete for them
Wanting my cake
and eat it, too

Well, why not?

WHAT PRICE GLORY

The financial manager is negotiating
    a new loan
I helped him with a strategy
    My son wants to drop out of school
But I come home too late at night
    to spend any time with him

The vice president in charge of production
    is not meeting schedules
I helped him plan
    My daughter is living with this guy
        I don't like
But I work on weekends and don't have time
    to talk to her

The lawyer is fighting an anti-trust suit
    I helped him write a brief
My spouse is leaving me
    because I'm never home
But I don't have the time to go on vacations

The sales force is not meeting forecasts
    I provided new incentives
The doctor says I must take it easy
    But I don't have the time . . .

I HAVE ARRIVED

I have not seen the plays in town
    only the computer print outs
I have not read the latest books
    only the Wall Street Journal
I have not heard birds sing this year
    only the sound of typewriters
I have not taken a walk anywhere
    but from the parking lot to my office
I have not shared a feeling in years
    but my thoughts are known to all
I have not shed a tear in ages
    but when I shout they tremble
I have not listened to my own needs
    but what I want I get
I have arrived —
    is <u>this</u> where I was going?

SUPPORT SYSTEMS

My right hand is being held
by someone who knows <u>more</u> than I,
and I am learning.
My left hand is being held
by someone who knows <u>less</u> than I,
and I am teaching.
So both my hands must thus be held
for me — to be.

WOMEN
and their
IMPORTANT
RELATIONSHIPS

PRIORITIES

We're working too hard
Accomplishing a lot but. . .
The time to play is passing us by.

We're in our separate worlds
Of creative concentration
It's wonderful but. . .
The time to be is passing us by.

We meet for meals
And speak of work
It's helpful but. . .
The time to know is passing us by.

We meet in bed
And go to sleep
It's restful but. . .
The time to love is passing us by.

SOCIALIZATION

Instead of minimizing our differences
Let us maximize them —
Instead of denying that you are better at this
but I am better at that
Let us take full advantage of our special skills
and recognize the weaknesses
in order to either work on them
or turn to what we do best.
It is OK with me
that most men have better spatial skills
and that most women are better at verbal skills
I can accept that most men are more concerned with objects
and most women with people
That boys excel at gross motor coordination
and girls at manual dexterity
That males are good at problem-solving
and females process information faster
I like our differences!
As you shovel the driveway
and I fix your hot soup
as you drive in the night
I keep you awake
as you carry the suitcases
I check in at the counter
you figure our taxes
I decide on our budget
you vacuum
I dust
you turn the mattress over
I water the plants
you chop the onions
I add the spices
you go marketing
but with my shopping list
you buy me books
I buy you ties
you know how to cure the ills of the world
I know how to cure your ills
you know what the children ought to do
I know how they are
you know about driving in the snow
I know you should wear a scarf
you show me how much you love me
I tell it to you
I could not do well what you do so well
nor could you do what I do
I like me as me
and you and you

RITUAL

Dim awareness
I'm waking up
He stirs too
We hug
and mumble:
how did you sleep
a question
not requiring
an answer
He turns the heat on in the house
I turn on the radio
we wait ten minutes
together in bed
sharing dreams
analyzing them
We exercise,
actually we dance
to fast music,
until out of breath
so much for our cardiovascular systems
I stretch
he does push ups
Then he shaves
I get breakfast
which I bring to bed
on two trays
The best time of the day is about to begin
to the sounds of our rushing stream
and with a view over our tree tops
through which squirrels do gymnastics
we have breakfast in bed
tea
sour dough whole wheat bread
and goat cheese
we try to eat slowly
to make the moment last

If I could change only one thing in my life
I would change my metabolism
so that I could eat breakfast all day

TRUST

I don't know
What is best for you
But I trust you to know that
I know
What is best for me
And I trust you
To trust me.

WAITING

He's late
it's dark
Supper is ready
he usually calls
I can't read
— too anxious
passing headlights
reflect in my window
I jump
it's him!
No.
maybe a car accident
a heart attack
a stroke
maybe he fell
he has an ID on him
they would call me
Do they call right away?
Who calls?
The police, the doctors?
Do they come personally
If it's terrible news?
The phone rings
I startle
it's him!
No.
I do my needle point
maybe it's the last happy minute of my life
because I don't know yet
Don't know the awful news
I will say afterwards:
I had this premonition.
I'm hungry
shall I eat without him
I better eat now
in case of bad news
I won't be able to later . . .
Oh God
I can't stand it
I hear the garage door
it's him!
Yes!!!

He had met this friend
and you know how it is . . .

TERRITORY

Are you more if I'm less
Do I breathe your air
Or fly in your space
When I take up more room
Do you become constrained
Do you value me more
When I'm beholden to you
Do you value me less
When I'm free and I soar
Are you less if I'm more

Adapted from "Woman to Man"
by J.R. Wells 8/77

HE/SHE

1. He brags about her body

   She brags about his job

2. He thinks she's cute

   She thinks he's strong

3. He wants her to look pretty

   She wants him to sound intelligent

4. He is proud of her running the house well

   She is proud of his position at work

5. He repairs

   She mends

6. He likes her deference

   She likes his dominance

7. He admires her knowledge of the arts

   She admires his knowledge of politics

8. He has the right answers

   She has the right questions

9. He couldn't manage without her

   She couldn't manage without him

   or could she?

THE EXECUTIVE'S WIFE

Company for dinner
his business associates
hors d'oeuvres
hot and cold
be sure to have
enough liquor in the house
enough soda
dress attractively
but not too
house should be clean
children out of the way
greet them smiling
chit-chat
don't talk business
if they do,
they'll apologize
for being boring
"I don't mind
in fact I'm interested"
polite smiles
nice home
lovely dinner
well-brought up children
becoming dress
charming wife
oh thank you
thank you for your favorable comments
on the house
    the dinner
    the children
    the dress
    the wife
(in that order?)
It was a <u>huge</u> success!

So why did the charming wife
           in her becoming dress
           with the well brought-up children
           and the lovely dinner
           in the nice home
           Leave?

FLOOR SCRUBBING

The 20s

He's a student   She's a student

They both scrub the floors

The 30s

He gets a job   She gets a baby

She scrubs the floors

He sometimes helps

The 40s

He gets promoted   She gets a job

She scrubs the floors

The 50s

He gets a presidency   She gets a maid

The maid scrubs the floors

The 60s

He retires   She gets promoted

He scrubs the floors

She sometimes helps

DISCRIMINATION

Because she's black
a funny shyness
about putting my arm
around her
as I would with a white woman
a reticence
about asking to touch
her thick hair
like I could with a white woman
a hesitation
about talking about being black
afraid to sound
like I'm prying
wanting to respect
her differentness
wanting to bridge it
wanting the sisterhood
with black women too
not sure of being accepted
of being acceptable

COOKING

I love to cook for him
special dishes he did not expect
I made a cheese sauce for the cauliflower
I put maple syrup in the squash
I poached the pears in wine
He expects only boiled, broiled or raw
and is very surprised by any extra specials
so that's why I make them
to surprise him
for this delights me

H idden in this poem
E ncapsulated in it, I
R evel in the sound of
M y love's name
A nd celebrate him
N ow and forever

HERMAN

He does not know
I'm watching him
standing in the bathtub.
I like his body
he's soaping himself
automatically
lost in his thoughts.
He has narrow hips
and a tender ass
a long thin torso
with a well-shaped head
full of thick hair
and a beautiful face
with loving blue eyes.
He stands very straight
and looks great in clothes —
but I like him naked
he feels more mine.

THE COUSIN FROM RUSSIA

For fifty years I corresponded
with a first-cousin in Russia
We started as small children
sending drawings to each other
and went to large letters
on lined paper;
to the sharing of adolescent dreams.
Her name was Natasha, like mine
we were the same age,
she also had red hair.
I imagined her beautiful,
exotic, and passionate.
She had her son
the year I had my daughter.
On a trip to Russia
our children met, years later.
They looked alike and got along
and then — the news
She had cancer and would die
The need to see each other once
To meet after all these years
I left for Moscow
she was at the airport
my beautiful young cousin
was a heavy-set middle-aged woman
with dyed hair and "Tzores"*

What did she see?
a short, grey-haired woman
just as middle aged!

*Yiddish word for "sorrows"

THE RUSSIAN SHAWL

I bought myself in Russia
this huge black shawl
with large red flowers
which made me feel like a gypsie:
I loved it.

While I was away
he gave it to his daughter
he said it was a mistake
he felt very badly about it!

I'm glad his daughter has it.
I'm sorry that I do not.
I'm angry he gave it away.
I'm guilty that I'm angry.
I told him it's O.K.
But it's not true
So I lied to make him feel better
but lying makes me feel worse
it isolates me
But I would rather feel badly
than make him feel badly
does all that make me a good person after all?

THE STEP-DAUGHTER

Tension in the air
Unease
I'm on my toes
My step daughter is visiting
I like her
That's not the issue
It's this tension in the air
After all these years
we still test each other
We evaluate
We are judgmental
Does it ever stop
Will we someday
take each other for granted
accept one another
as women of the same family
I hope so
But I don't know
how to make it happen
now

WHEN I'M FULLY IN CHARGE OF ME

When I'm fully in charge of me
   I can let you too be free.

When I am using my fullest potential
   I can help others do the same.

When I am empowered and strong and sure
   I feel neither envious nor threatened.

When I can grow at my own rate
   I do not fear your taking anything away.

I do not fear your overtaking me.

ACCESSIBILITY

Father is taking a nap.
His door is closed.
Children tip toe
and whisper.
Sh, Father's asleep.

Mother is taking a nap.
Her door is open
so she can hear
children fight or cry.
Mothers never take
Real naps.

GRADUATION

Twenty-two years at the same job
including evenings and weekends.
No vacation time to speak of
and now it's done:
PROJECT SUCCESSFULLY COMPLETED!

Yet, no farewell party,
no inscribed medal,
not even a watch
to commemorate a full time job
held for twenty-two years
with very little complaint.

There had been no grievance procedures,
no upward mobility,
no horizontal enrichment,
no lateral moves
and mostly vicarious rewards.

While everyone is pleased,
no one is particularly grateful.
It is normal it seems
that while they get their pictures taken
I once more just do the applauding.

THE DISPLACED HOMEMAKER

They ate the food I cooked for them.
They wore the clothes I washed.
They slept in the beds I made.
Spent money they did not earn.

I took them to their lessons.
Drove them to visit their friends.
Put their teeth in braces.
Enrolled them in summer camp.

I helped them with their homework.
Told stories, taught them songs.
Insisted on good manners.
and cried when things went wrong.

I listened to their problems.
Settled their disputes.
Nursed them when they sickened
and cuddled them a lot.

Now that they do not need me
now that they're on their own,
I have earned a brand new label.
As "displaced homemaker" I'm known.

THE FIFTH WHEEL

Why is it
that when a woman alone
is invited by a couple
it's charity
and she's grateful
but when a man alone
is invited by a couple
it's fun
and he takes it for granted.

Why is it
that two women and one man
is one woman too many
but two men and one woman
is a trio.

It is because we assume
that if he is alone
it is out of choice
and if she is alone
it is because
no one asked her?

BORN YESTERDAY

We have moved
New neighborhood
New job
New friends

We must create a history
So that we can have a past
With every move
We are born yesterday
All over again
With no shared memories

I want to push the time
To bridge the gaps
Knowing others
Being known by them
I want instant friendship
Instant love, care, trust

I want in the new place
All I have lost in the old
Without having to earn the stripes
Of having to prove
I really am a worthwhile person
Nor going through the rites of passage
Of hoping to be accepted
And trying to please

I am not sure
I will pick up the cues
Understand the humor
Be "in"
Be "part of"
Be "with it"
In the new neighborhood
At the new job
With the new friends

MIRACLES WILL NEVER CEASE

From one author
to another,
From a mother to a son,
From pride in my book
to more pride in yours,
From formerly ignorant mother
now professor of management
To formerly dyslexic son,
now successful author,
I send you three cheers,
two hip hip hurrahs,
and the hugest congratulations.

FIRST GRANDCHILD

Over 3,000 miles away from me
There is a child in Canada
A brand new child
And here in my solar plexus
There is this new joy
That is like an old pain
Which I recognize:

The vulnerability
Of loving so much
Of caring so much
Of worrying about another person now
For the rest of my life

I don't know her yet
But we are inextricably bound for ever
My new grandchild and I.

MIRACLES

My daughter
Has a daughter

I have a granddaughter

My mother is a great grandmother

All miracles

FOR LAURA

Size 1 month, please
With matching booties in pink and blue
Laura's first dress

A soft teddy bear, please
With a music box inside
Laura's first toy

And a grandmother
Far, far away is writing
Laura's first poem

WOMEN
ALONE

TODAY'S WOMEN

We are
Today's women
Born yesterday
Dealing with tomorrow

AMBIVALENCE

When I am home doing nothing
I wish I were out doing something
Something exciting, of course!

But when I am out doing something
And I am harried or anxious
I wish I were home doing nothing.

When I'm at my job in the office
I wish I were home with the children
Missing them, worried and guilty.

But when I am home with the children
I am so bored or impatient
That I wish I were back in the office.

EXHAUSTION

I'm exhausted!
So I drink all this coffee
it makes my heart pound
but I'm just as exhausted.

so I eat all this chocolate
it makes me fat
but I'm still exhausted

so I take a nap
it makes me listless
and no less exhausted

so I take a walk
I can hardly drag myself around the block
it didn't help either

so I'm writing this poem
it helped . . .

TIME OUT

A grey day in November
too warm for a chimney fire
too cold to go out

Too much work to play
but not quite enough
to preclude day-dreaming

A hot cup of tea
with a lemon slice
A spoon of brown sugar
a clove, a nutmeg
a cinnamon stick
and just a little bit of rum

Ah —

THE OYSTER RIVER

The first night in the new house
we thought it was raining
but it had not
the second night we heard again
the sound of water falling
but all was dry outside.

The river had swelled
from the melting spring snows
just under our window
a small rushing water fall
was splashing over rocks

The river was fast
bumping along big tree stumps
as it flowed downstream
it was deep enough
to drown me
and maybe thirty feet wide

Then the summer came
and the river trickled
we could not hear it at night
as we walked across it easily
and fished in the quiet pools

The fall laid leaves on it
and I watched them sail slowly by
the river was narrow
with only six feet
to the other side

The winter iced it completely
except for one pool near the rocks
when the snow falls over the river
we cross country ski its full length
from Mill Road to the Mill Pond

Every morning before breakfast
I check if it is still there
and with floodlights after sunset
we can still watch it in the dark

The river has become a presence
someone who lives with us
when people come to visit
we say
oh, come look at our river today!

6:00 A.M.

6:00 A.M.
I listen to the Maine news
To make sure the weather is OK
he took the plane from Portland today.
I turned on the TV
these women look like evening
at 6:00 in the morning
I would not want their jobs.
And now I sit in bed
listening to the quiet
New Hampshire is a quiet state.
I strain my ear for a sound
none —
how extraordinary in our times
to hear nothing
and to feel peace!
I am totally happy
and feel privileged
to be looking forward to a whole day alone.
Alone in my house
to do as I please
I please to write all day today
in the quiet and peace of my house.
How wonderful
that I have all day
to think and to write.
I write this poem
as a prayer of thanks
at 6:00 this morning
at the start of my special quiet day.

CHRISTMAS HOLIDAY

I did it again
The wrong resort
I tried to save money
All pre-paid of course
It's not South enough
The water is too cold
The waves are too high
The pool is too small
The beach is crowded
and I'm unhappy
Dreaming of warm lagoons
Where I'm not
So
I walked on the beach
Sat in the sun
Read a lot
and came back well rested

FALLING SNOW

What is there to see
in the endless flakes
which has not
already been seen

What is there to hear
in the muffling of sounds
which has not
already been heard

What is there to feel
about a winter storm
which has not
already been felt

What is there to write
about falling snow
which has not
already been said

Only one thing:
I stay too long at the window
unable to tear myself away
with renewed awe and endless wonder
I always watch the falling snow

T.V.

Sometimes in the evening
I'm so tired
I can't read
I can't write
I can't talk
I can't think
and it's too early
to go to sleep
so I watch TV
sitting in bed
but I still
feel guilty
that I'm not
being constructive
(whatever that is)
But where is it written
that it's not O.K.
to waste time
and anyway
what's wasted time
if I enjoy it
then it's not wasted
by definition

SORCELLERY

For "knowledge"
you get acclaimed
    prizes — promotions

For "knowing"
you get burned
    fantasies — fears

"Knowledge" is a public fact
up front
You either have it or you don't
And all can see

"knowing" is a private experience
hidden
If you know and don't tell
It won't show

White men in their heads
possess the Knowledge
Women, Blacks in their guts
have the Knowing

Warlocks, black men, black magic
weaving spells
witches, hags, fortune tellers
casting curses

Burn them all for their knowing
for their secret and fearful powers
    Only "Knowledge" will be allowed here.

GODS & DEMAGOGUES

The gods of yesteryear
Appeased by human sacrifice
Today, too,
Nothing less will do
To appease the demagogues

IMAGES

Close your eyes and listen
Down the hollowed halls of academe
Walks the professor
Whom do you hear?
A man?

Bent over musty manuscripts
In dank cellars of old libraries
Studies the scholar
Whom do you see?
A man?

In a well-lit office
Behind a large desk
Sits the administrator
Who is it?
A man?

Open your eyes and ask
Why never a woman?

CREDENTIALS AND WISDOM

When you acquire knowledge
You get credentials
When you acquire experience
You get wisdom
You can have one <u>without</u> the other
Knowledge is in books
        in classrooms
        in conferences
        in research
Experience is in living
You can have credentials when you're young
You can have wisdom when you're old
Studying gives you credentials
Life gives you wisdom
So if I live long enough and study hard
I will have <u>both</u>

INFLATION

The more I can earn

The less I can buy

HOW TO EAT A POMEGRANATE

Don't have arthritis in your hands
cup the fruit in your palms
squeeze with your thumbs
all around and around
you'll hear the seeds crackle
pierce with a sharp knife
in the kitchen sink
because it spurts
suck the juice
while squeezing
'til it looks
like an empty pouch

REAL ESTATE

As prices go up
So do my hopes
    of owning a house
Go up in smoke, that is

UNAFRAID

If I am small and weak
Then I act big and strong
Lest I be found out
And not be loved

When I am big and strong
Then I can ask for help
Unafraid of what they will think
Unafraid to seem weak
Unafraid . . .

TOKENS

The only woman at the meeting
the only black in the group
the older person with the young folk
the homosexual
the least educated
the poorest
the handicapped
the only Jew
the recently widowed

Survival is in the finding of kindred spirits
anywhere
Finding support in
the Women's Movement
The Black Caucus
the Grey Panthers
the widow's group
the gay community
Finding support
where one can cry
or explode
or just be oneself
without representing
the women's point of view
or the black culture
or the Jewish people
or the aged.

We need a place
not to be one down
but to be equal
a place where we are not different
for a little time at least
a place we can trust the others
a place where we don't fear
the racists
the sexists
the anti-semites
the elitists
where you don't have to be a couple to be invited out
or straight
or young and beautiful
a place of our own
with a people of our own

Just in order
to survive.

WHAT AM I

Somewhere between always giving to others
and always keeping it all to myself
I stand
Somehow between only caring for others
and only caring for me
I live
But when I am only for others
I ask
Who will be for me
and when I am only for me
Then what am I?

Adapted from Hillel, Aboth 1:14
The Talmud of Babylon

PLUMS & PRUNES

Your skins are taut
Your faces smooth
    like fresh plums

My skin is wrinkled
My brow furrowed
    like a prune

Prunes are sweeter

I am my
sister's
keeper!

I AM MY
SISTER'S
KEEPER!